CAT ROYALE
The Royal Cat Coloring Book

Volume 1

CREATED BY: GULLIVER PARASCANDOLO
PUBLISHED BY: CAT ROYALE BOOKS
COPYRIGHT © 2020

This Book Royally Belongs To:

_____

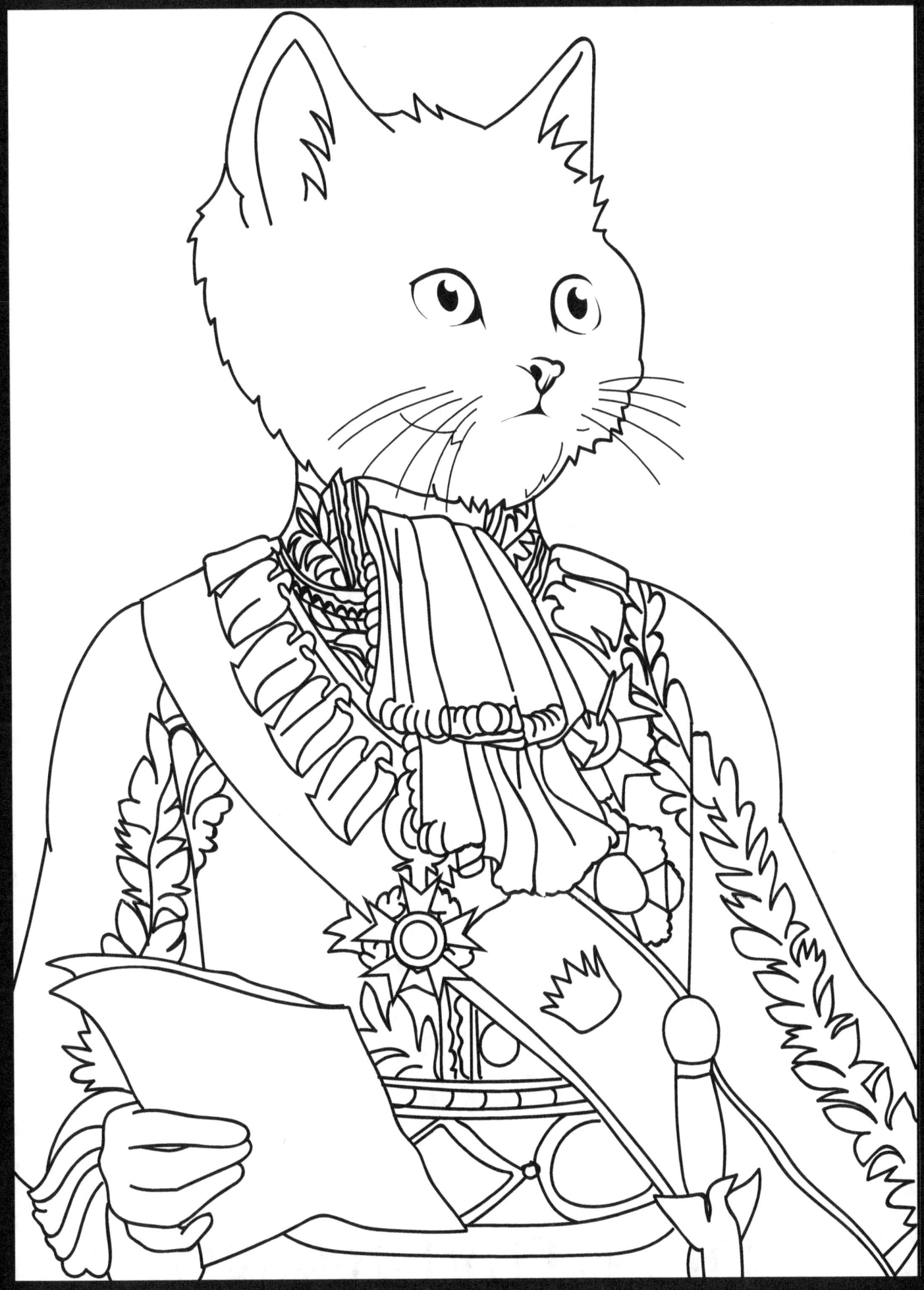

DUKE FURDINAND

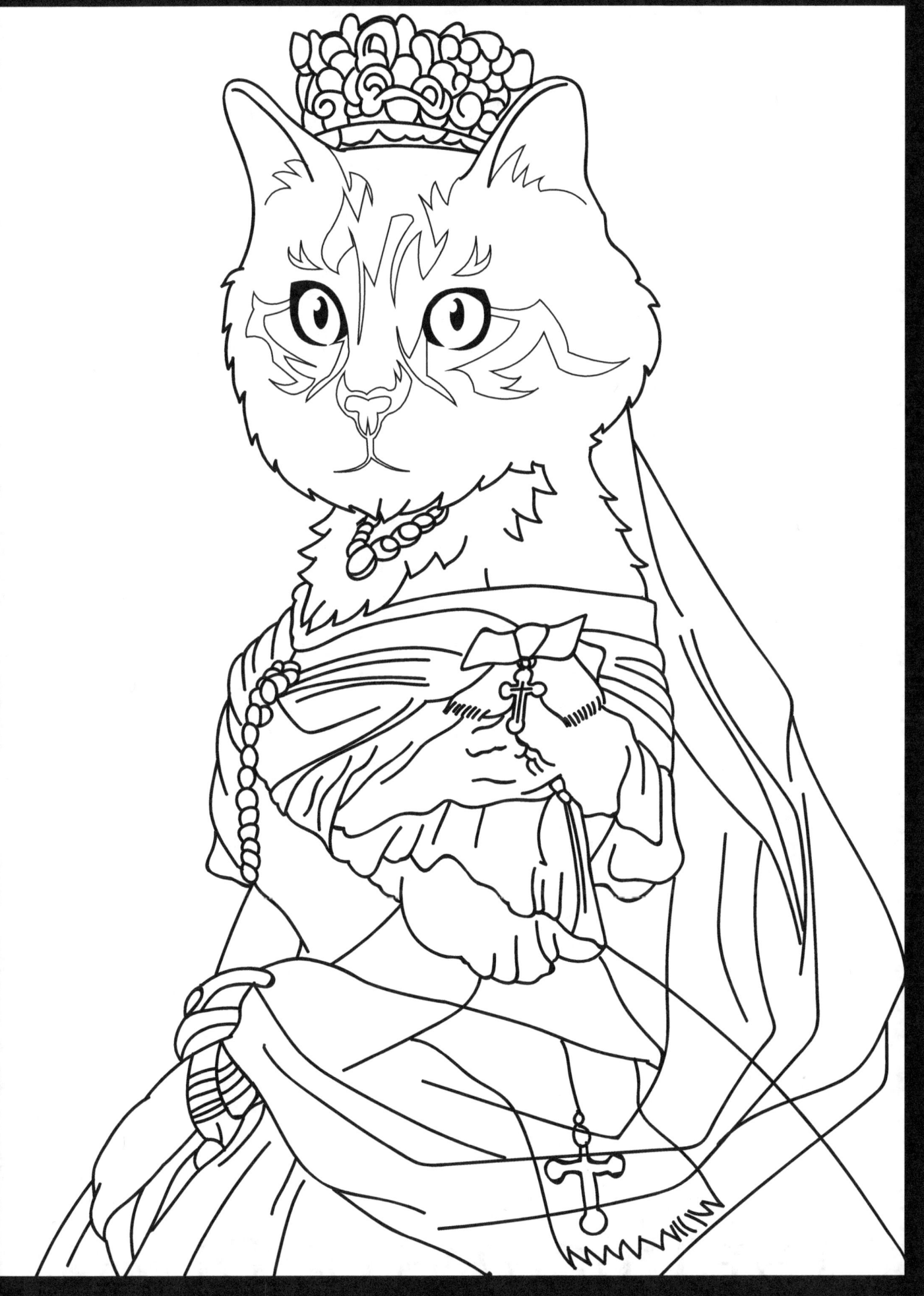

The Duchess of Dukes

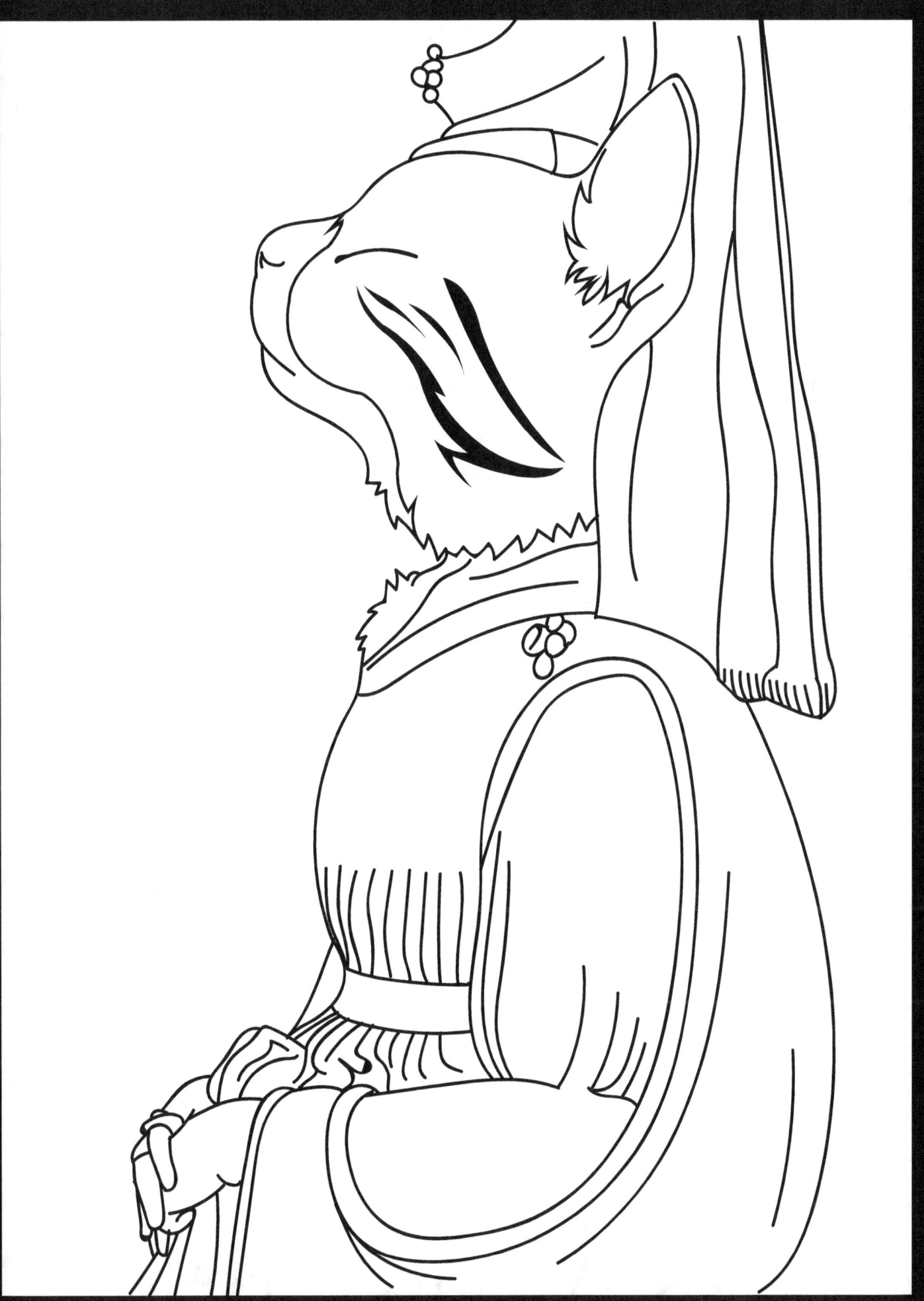

LADY TABBYTHA

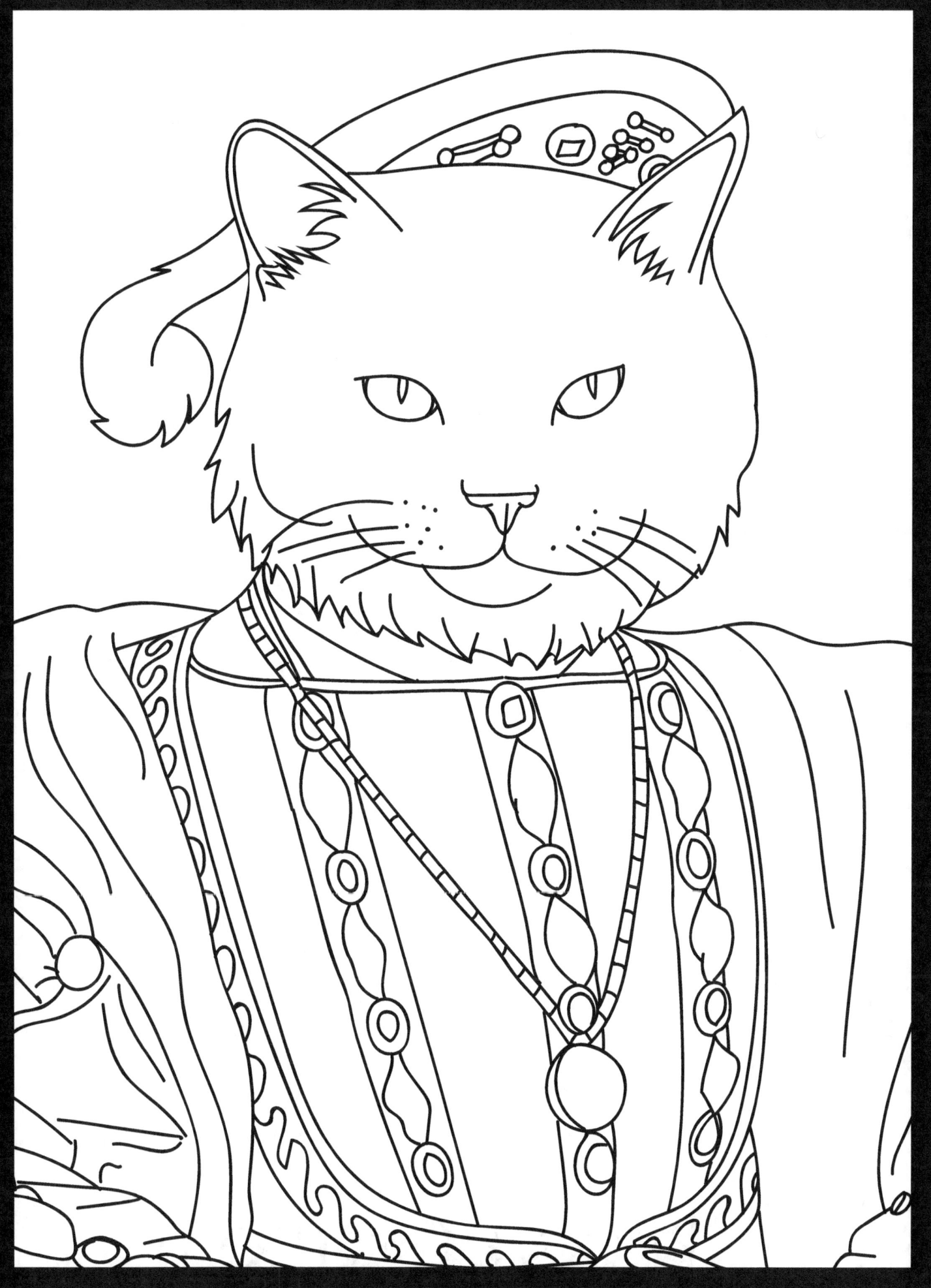

PRINCE CALICO

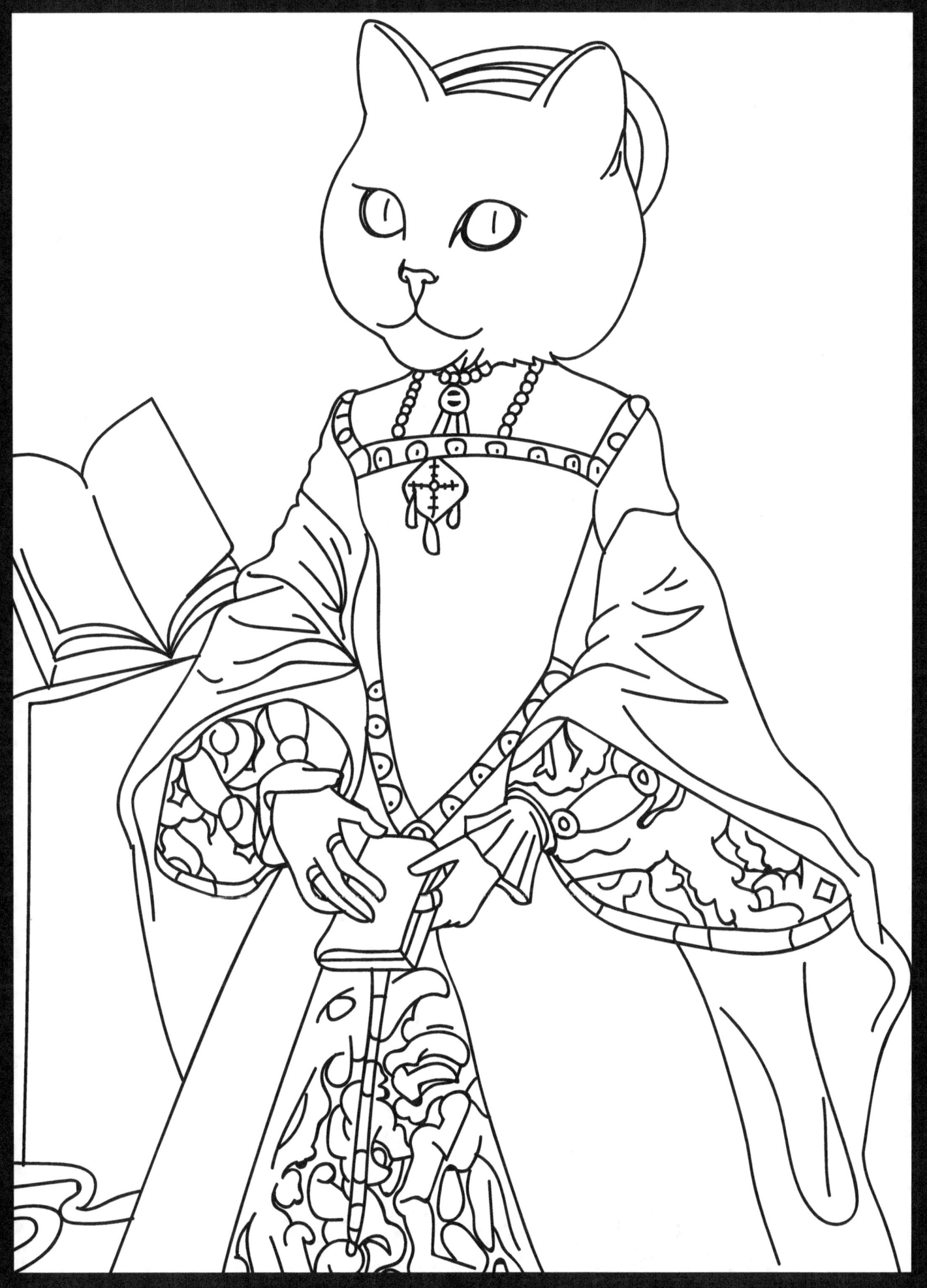

QUEEN PETITE

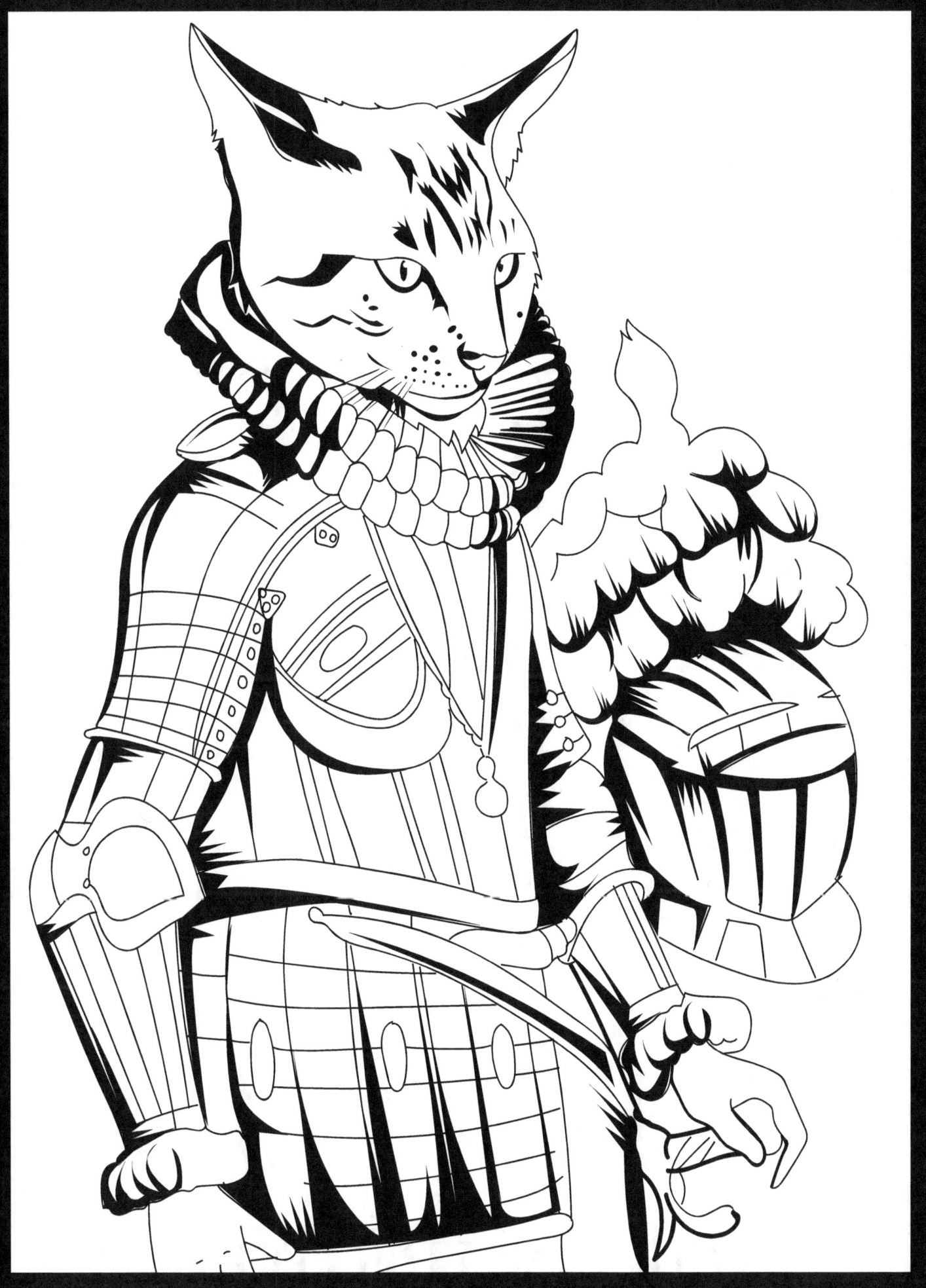

SIR CATTINGTON

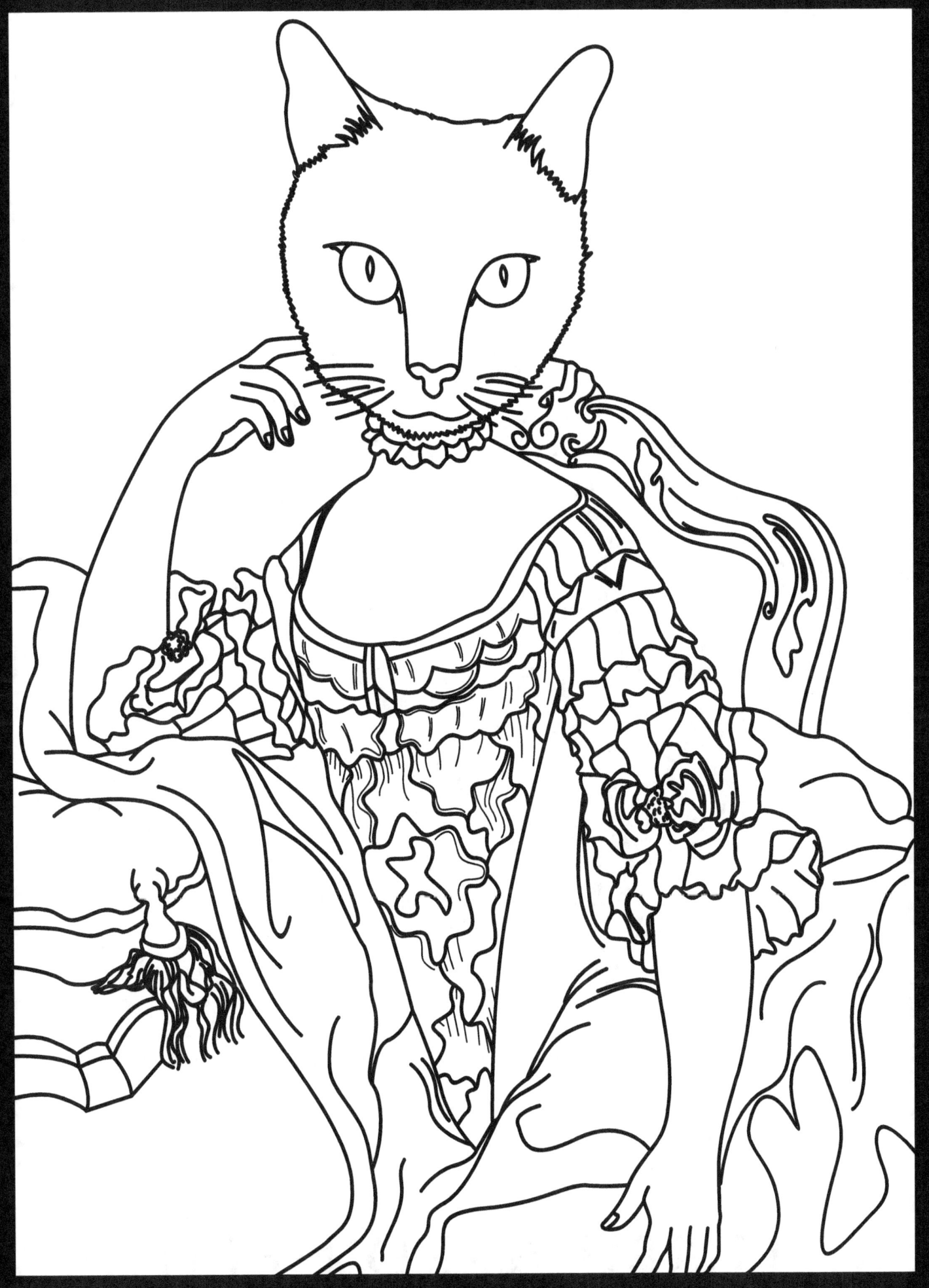

Furrie Antoinette

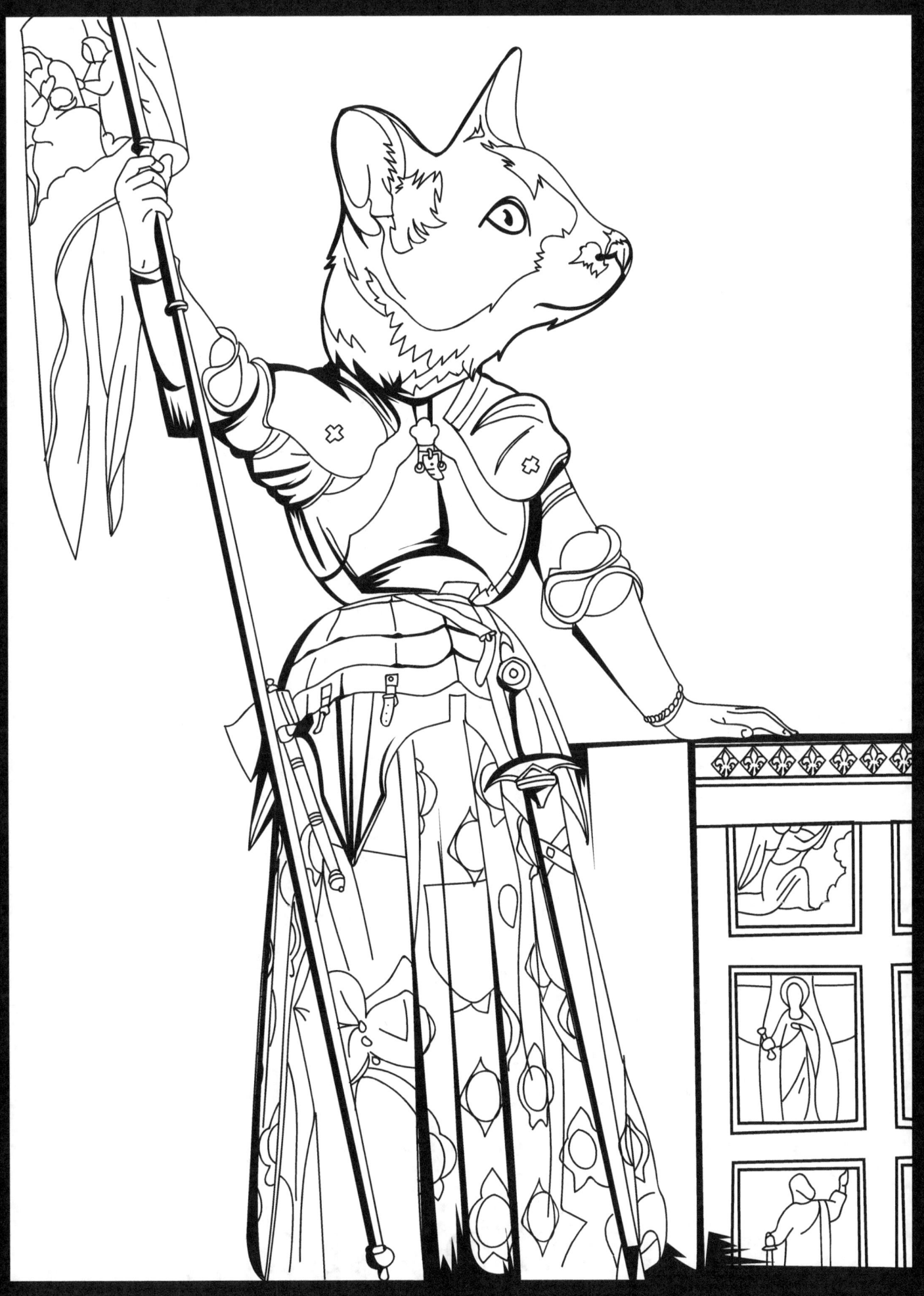

JOJO OF ARC

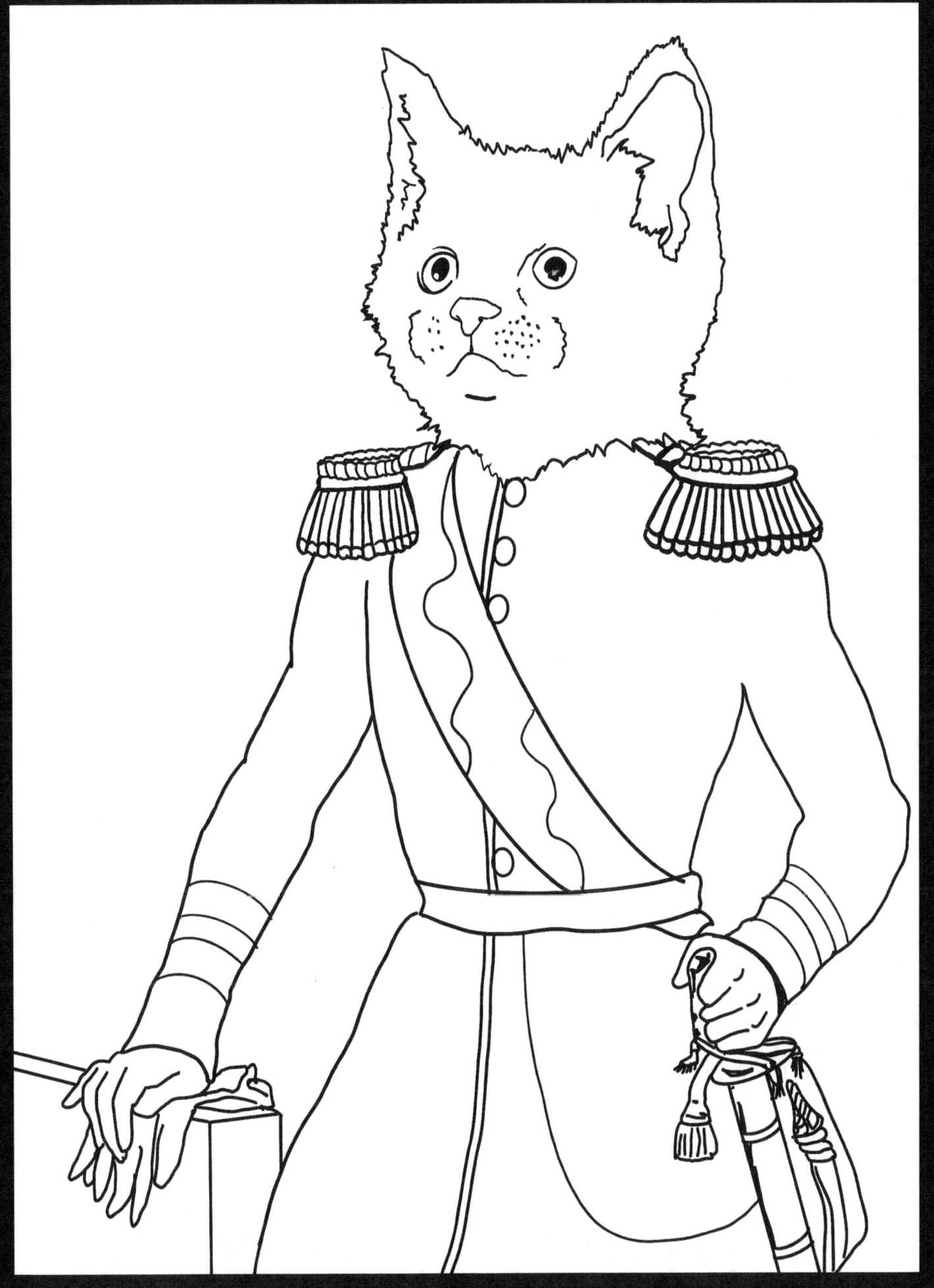

LORD SWIFTFOOT

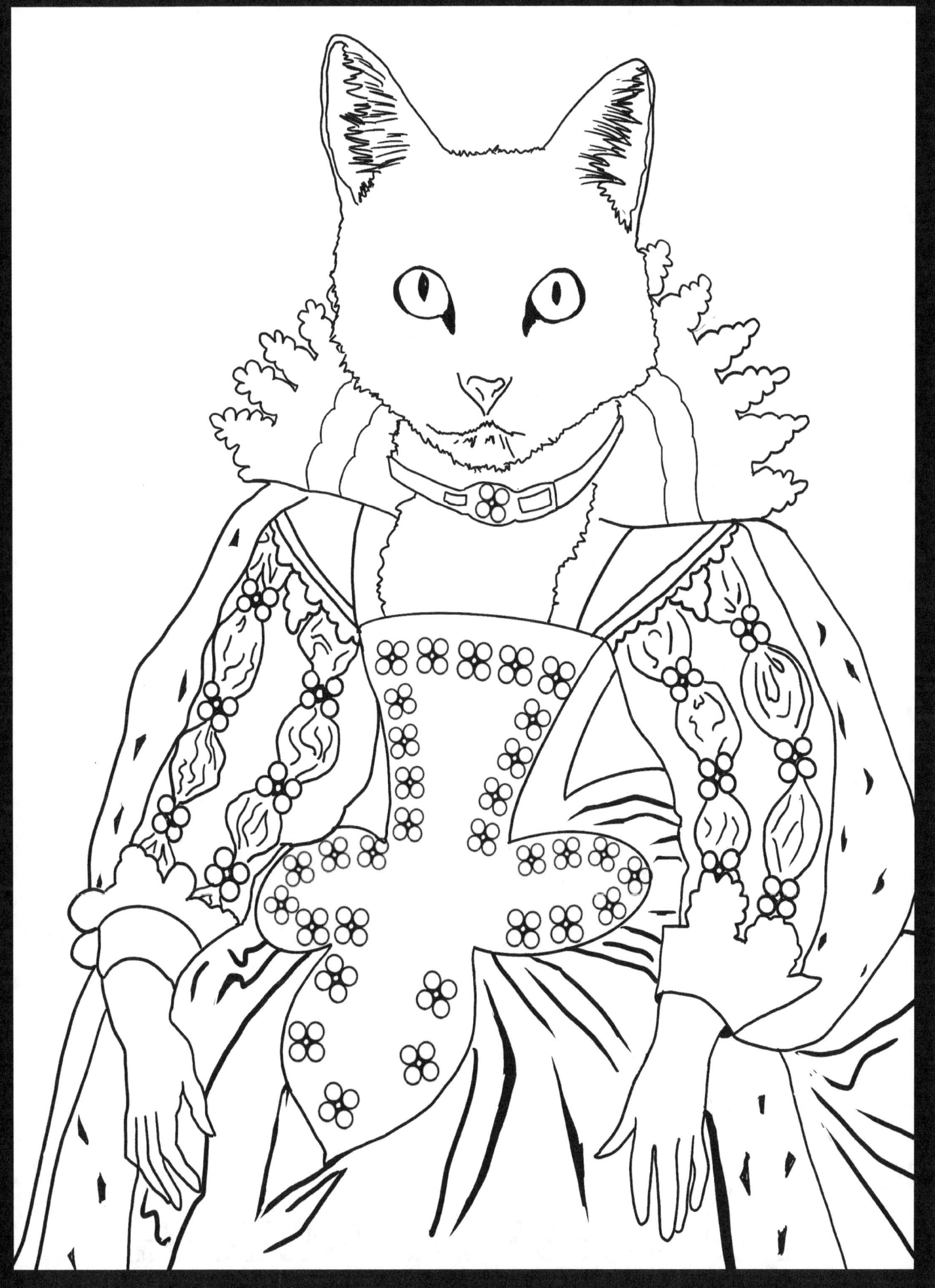

PRINCESS PAWMERAH

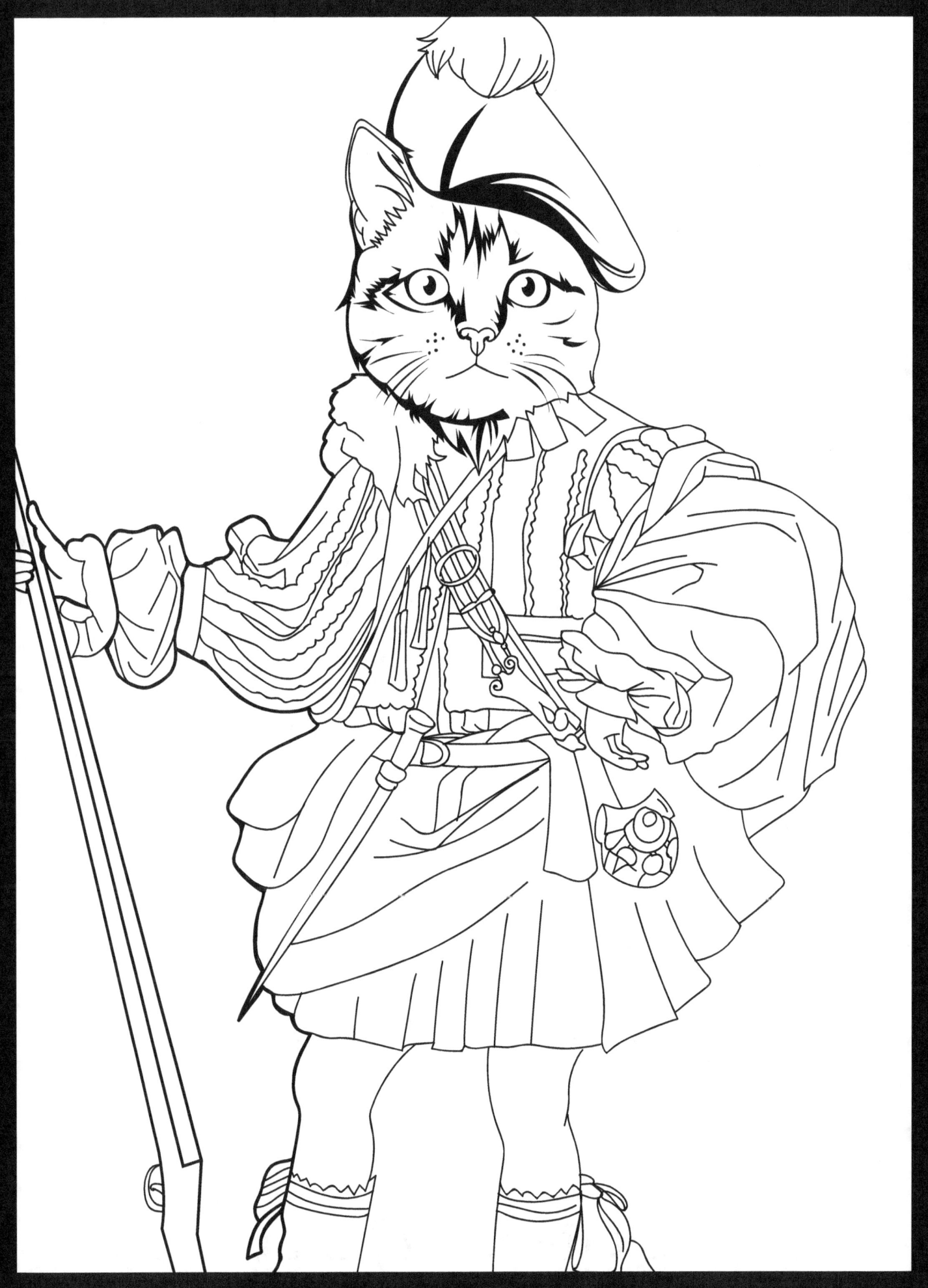

DON CATJOTE

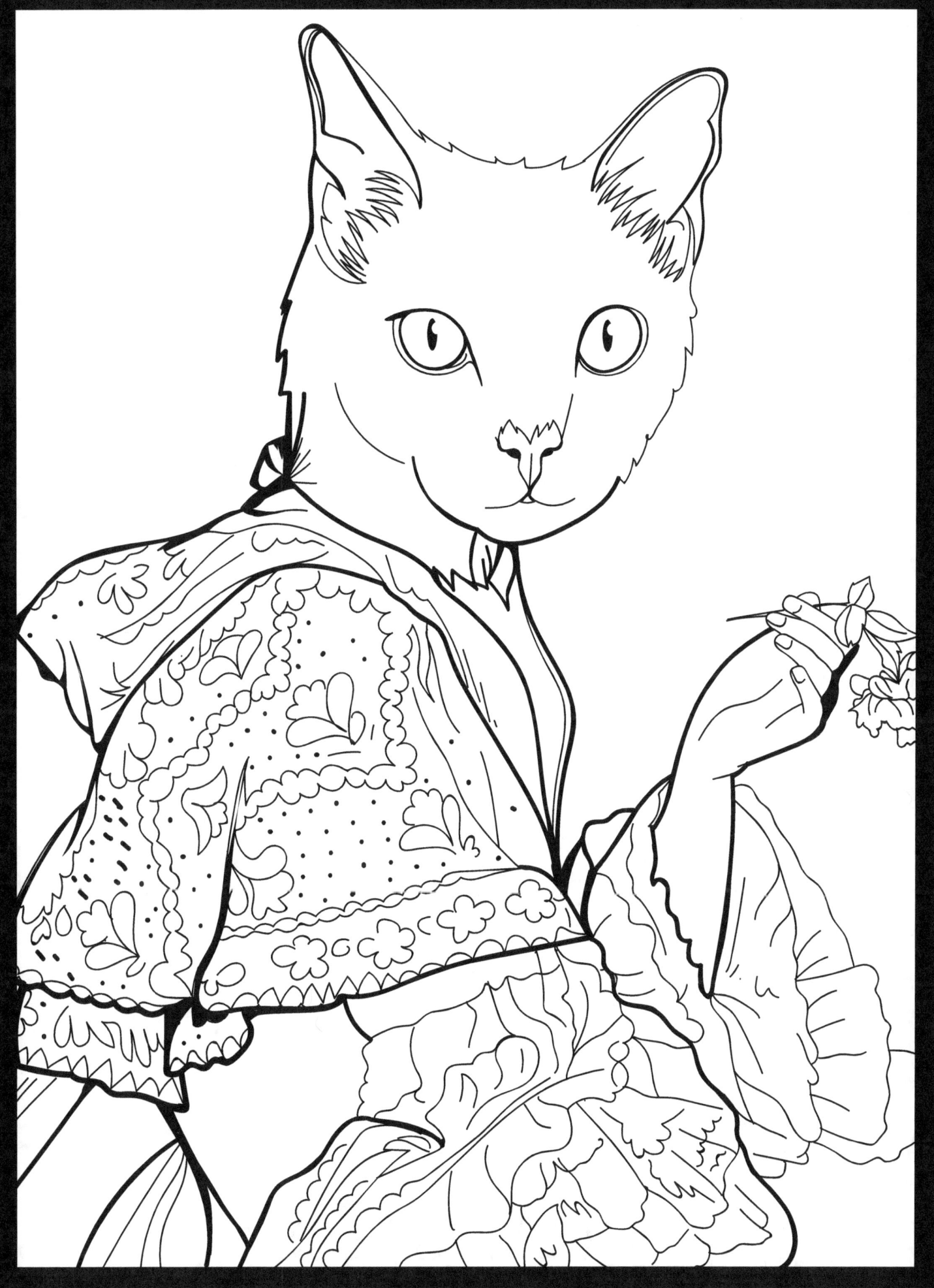

Queen Sheeba

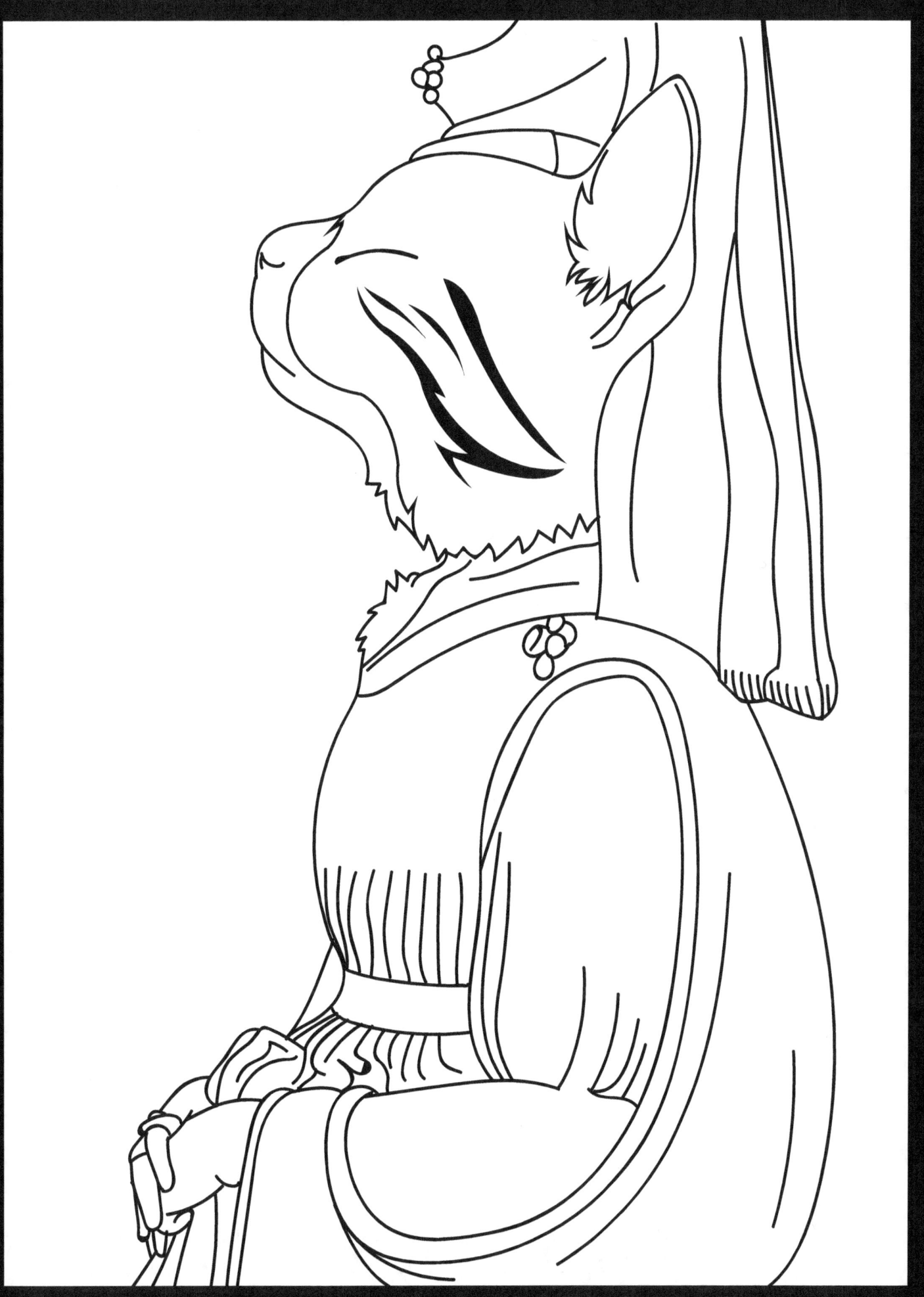

Maid Meowian

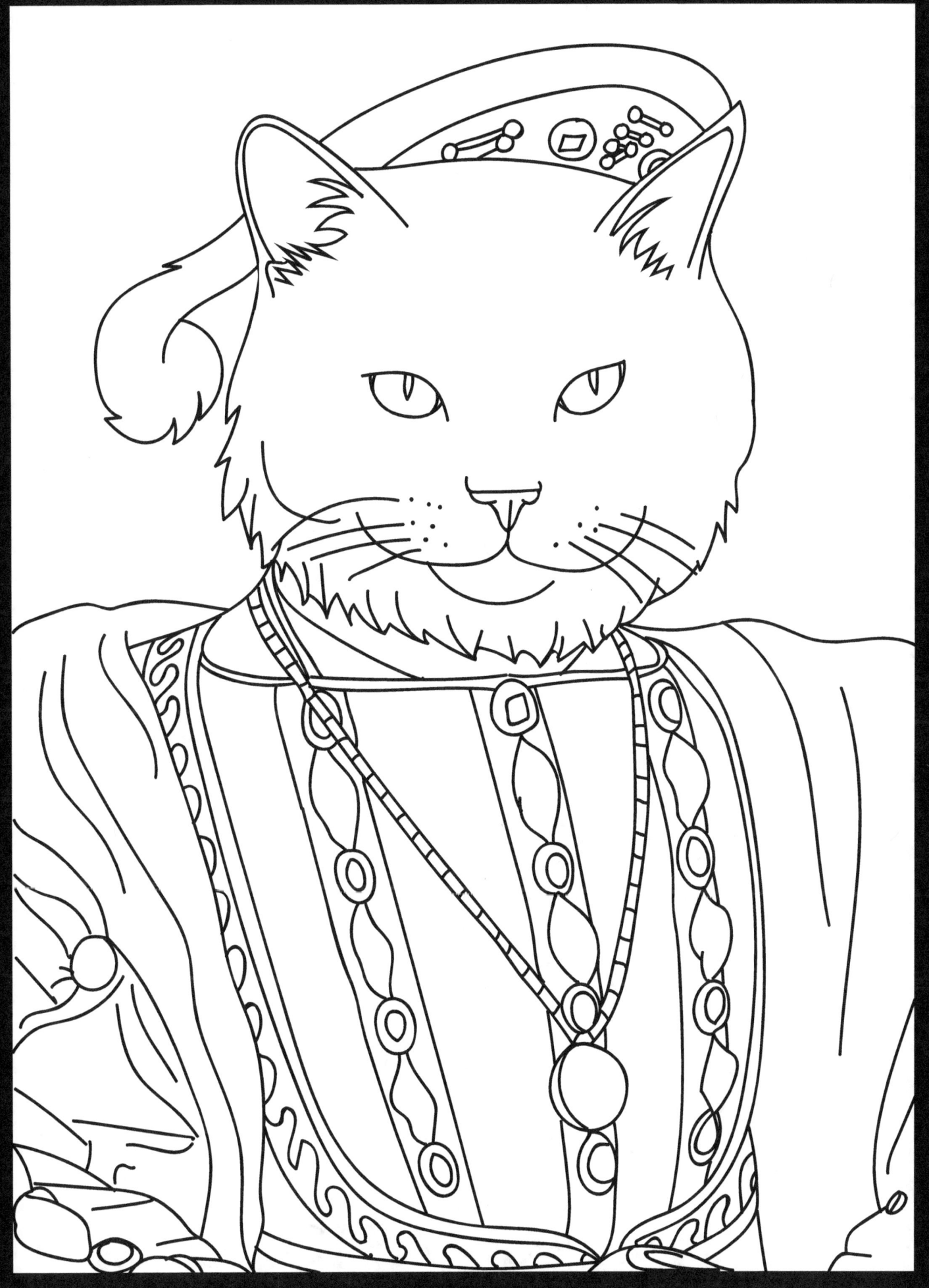

Purrcasso

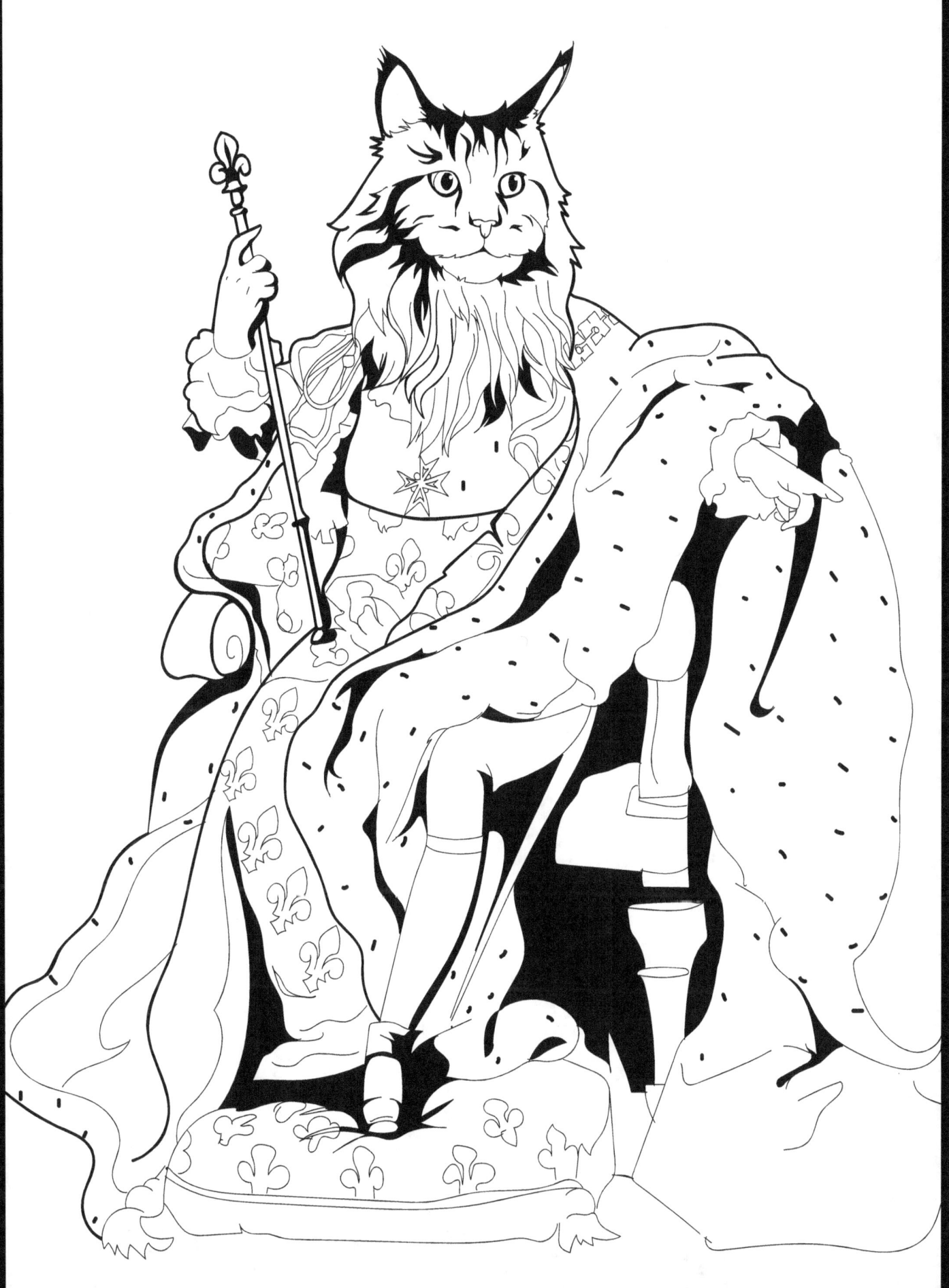

DUKE TABBYWORTH

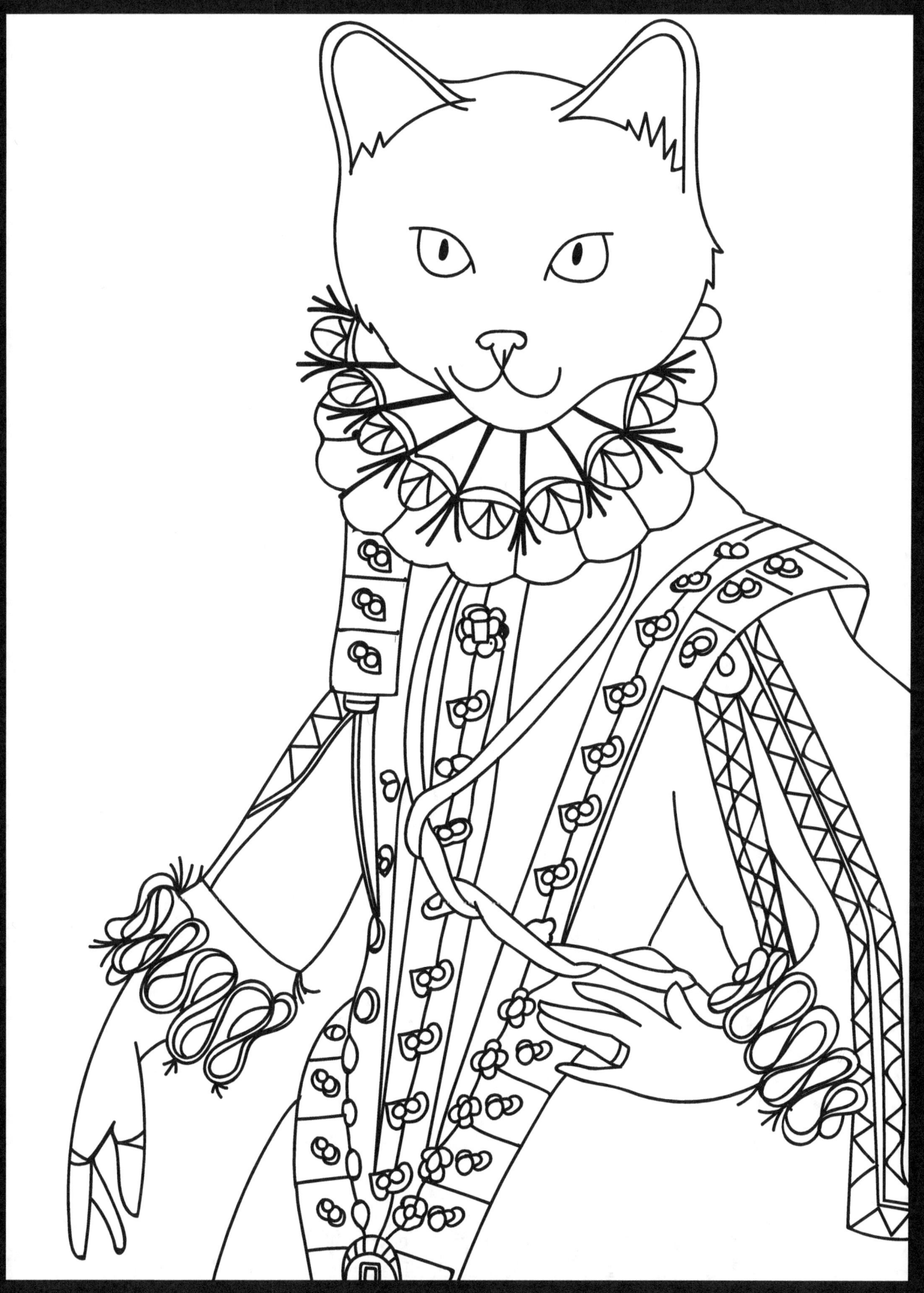

Catina the First

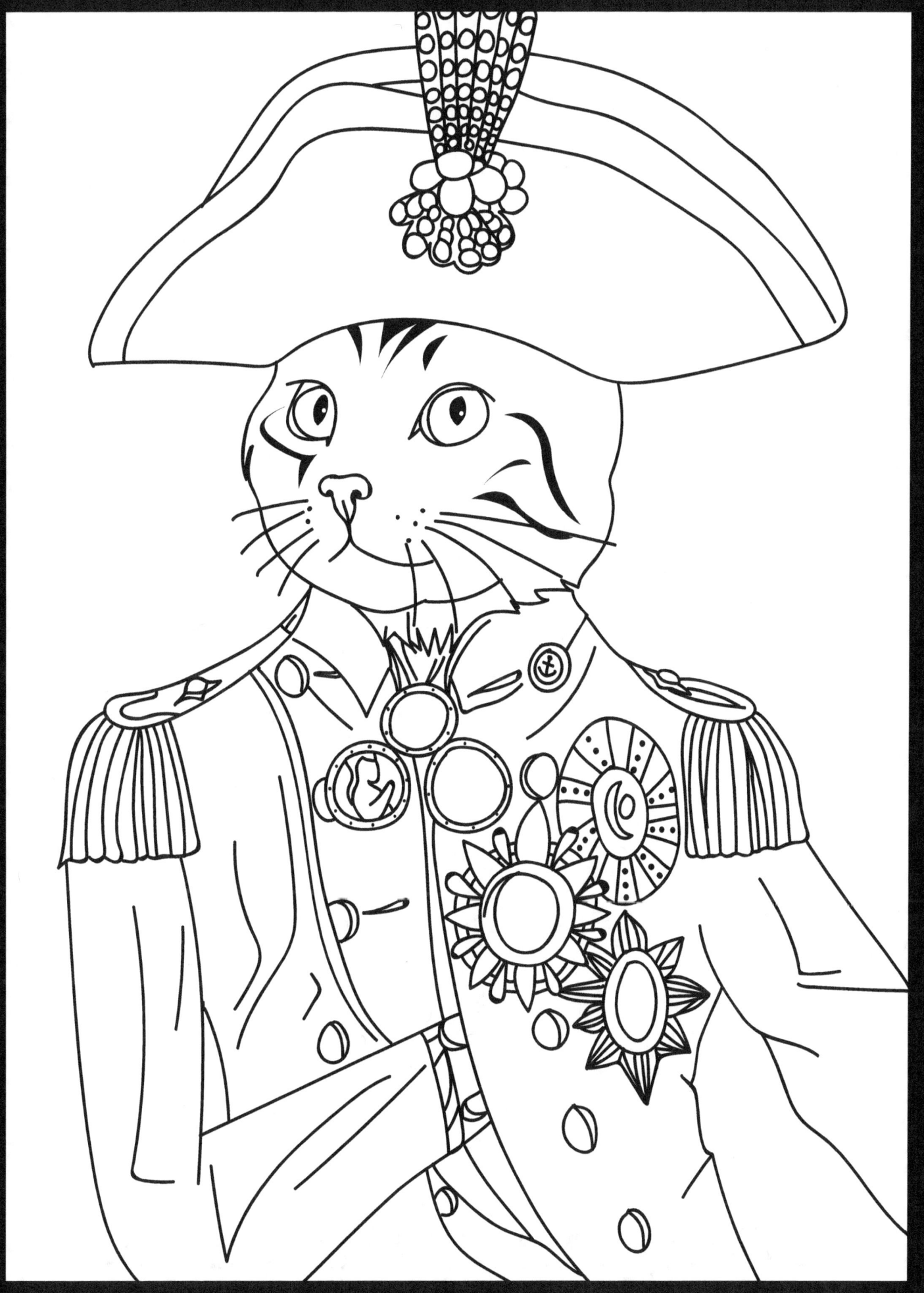

LORD PURRTHINGTON

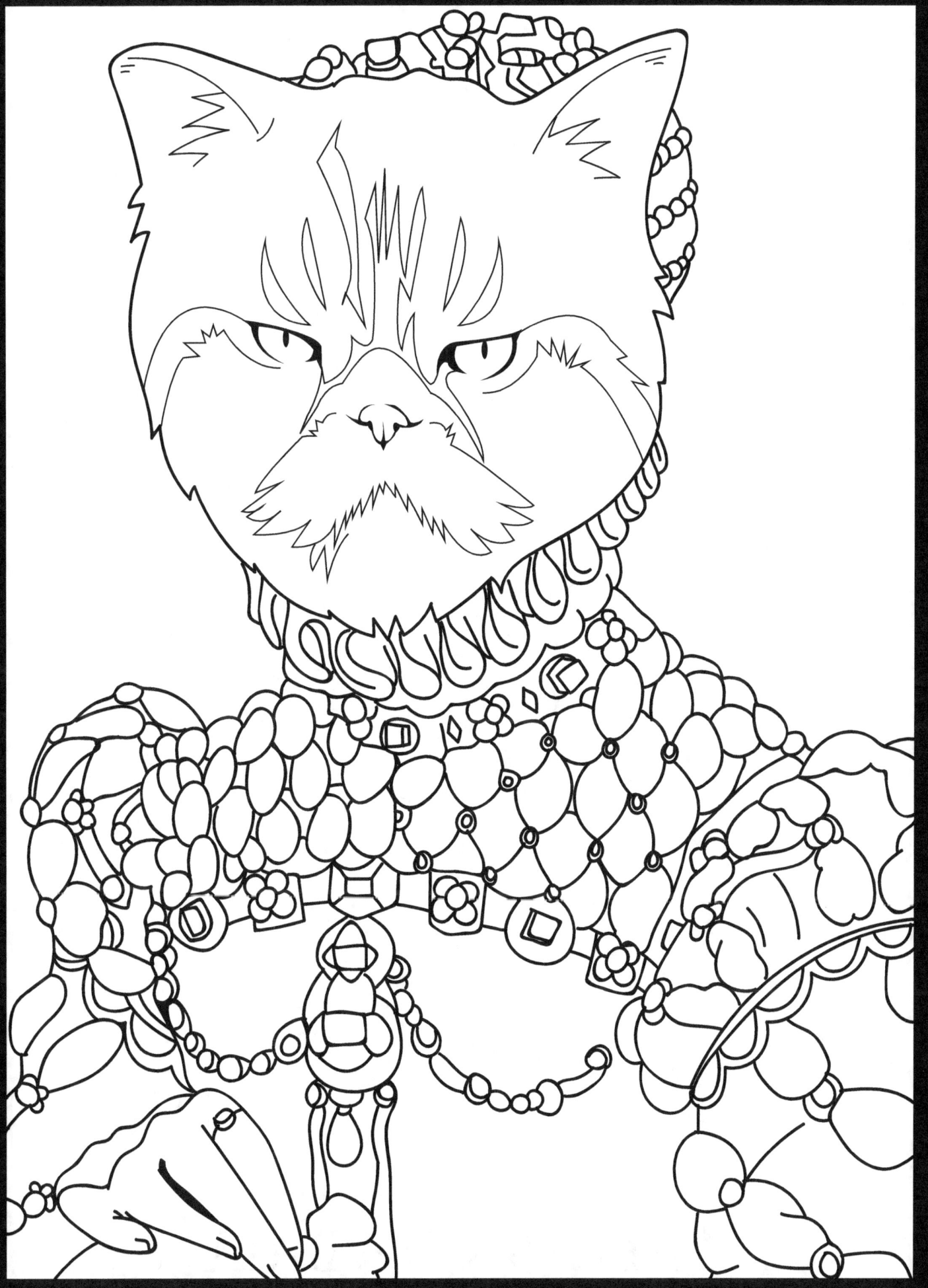

LADY SNOWBALL

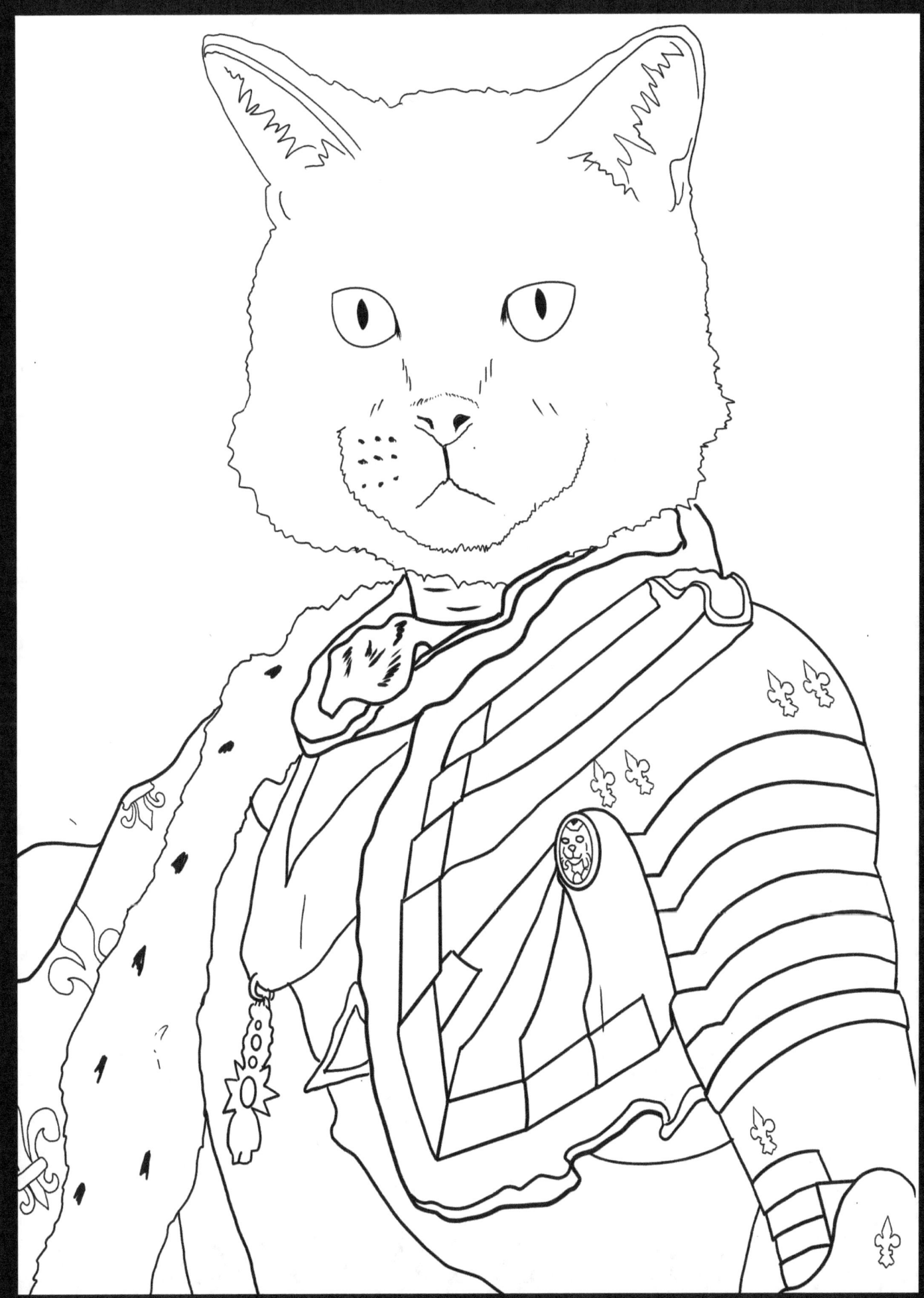

SIR LUIS DE GATO

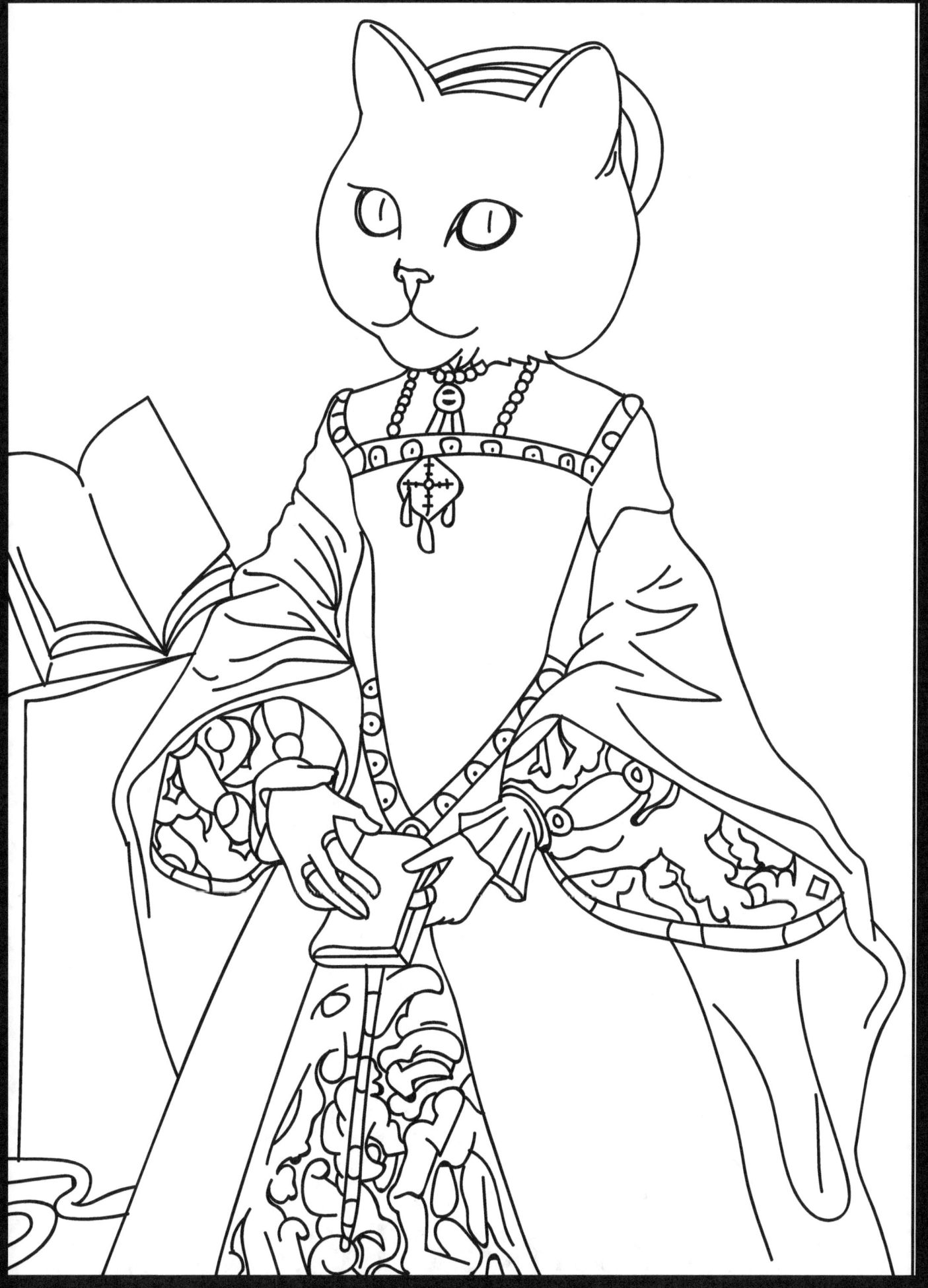

PRINCE LEO

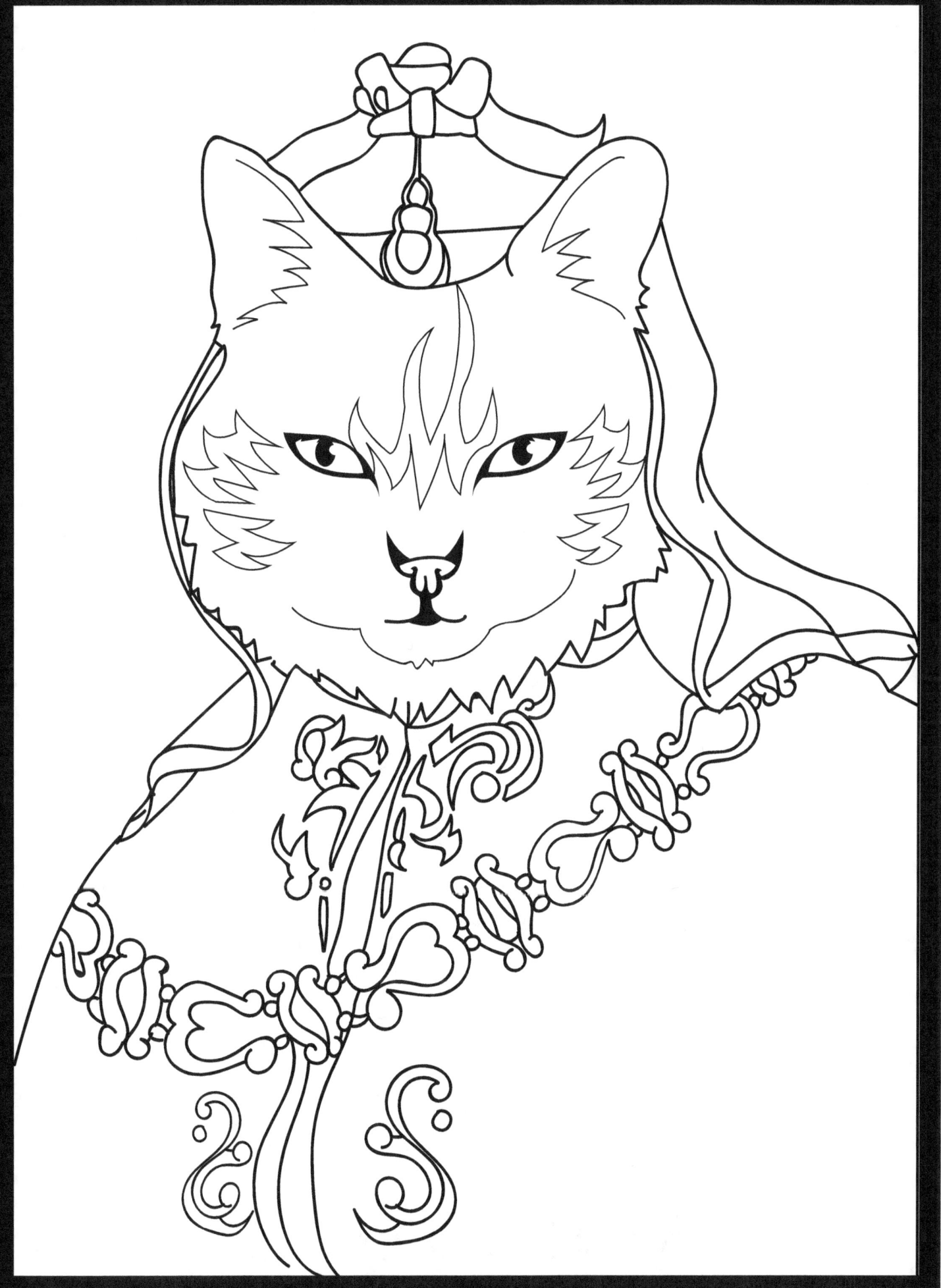

KING LIONOH

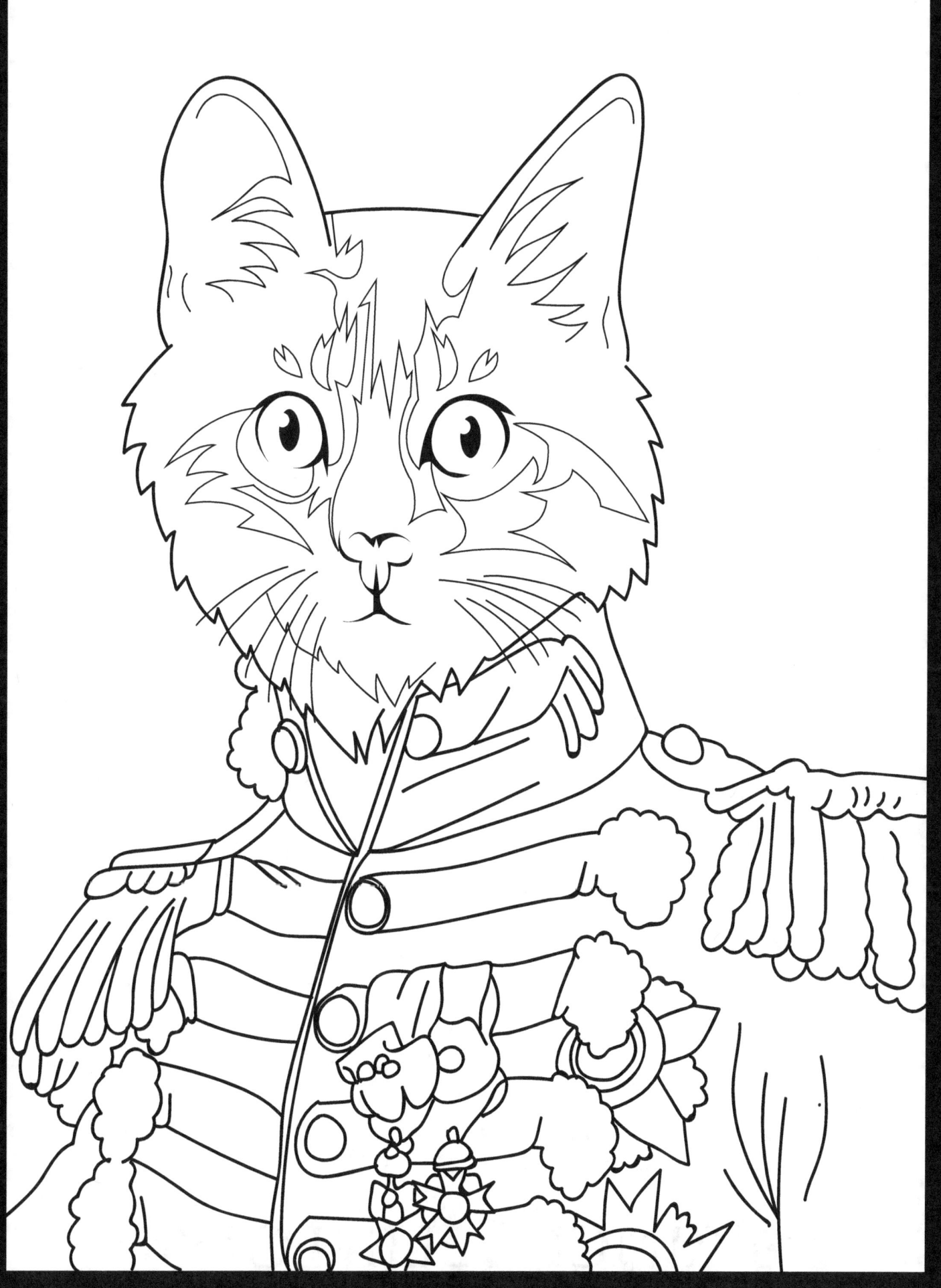

PRINCE FELINEOUS

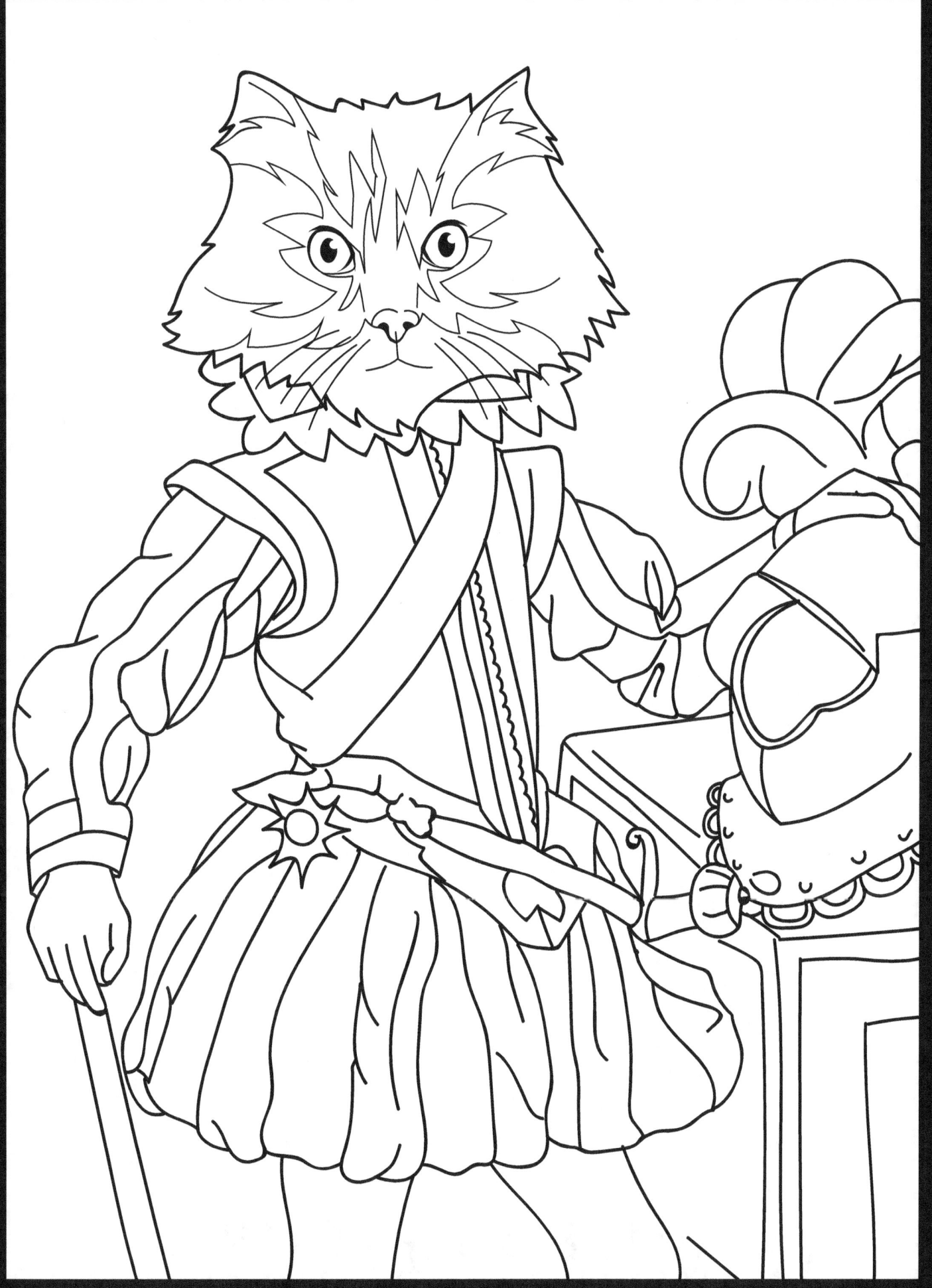

Sir Long Hair

www.ingramcontent.com/pod-product-compliance
Lightning Source LLC
Chambersburg PA
CBHW081059240526
45465CB00025B/2756